What people are saying about

What Do Quakers Believe?

The clearest introduction to Qu... ...y
and clearly written, this book bri... ...to life in a very
accessible way.

Nick Baines, Bishop of Leeds, broadcaster and writer

It is not easy to explain what Quakers believe; we are notoriously hard to pin down. Yet Geoffrey Durham has managed to unpack Quakerism in an open, lucid and friendly way. If you have ever wondered what is actually happening in a room full of people sitting in silence together, you will understand better after reading *What Do Quakers Believe?* – and may want to try it yourself. It is a book even Quakers can benefit from. Reading it also made me understand myself better – how I'm put together, how I operate in the world, and – yes – what I believe.

Tracy Chevalier, bestselling author of *Girl With a Pearl Earring* and *The Last Runaway*

In this excellent and informative book Geoffrey Durham explains in direct and straightforward language who the Quakers are and what they believe. Quakers reject no one. They have a deep respect for human life and for the world in which we live and they attempt to bring some common sense to a world that is increasingly driven to distraction in the endless pursuit of "bigger and better". I warmly commend this book to you. It caught my attention from the very first page.

Terry Waite CBE, bestselling author of *Taken on Trust* and *Solitude: Memories, People, Places*

"If you look to Quakers for a belief system you are going to be disappointed," writes Geoffrey Durham. But he certainly does not disappoint in the clarity he brings to portraying the shared principles by which Quakers seek to live and act. The pages of this book are powered by the potential for change – in individuals and in the world.

Mike Wooldridge OBE, former religious affairs journalist and broadcaster

What do Quakers Believe?

Quaker Quicks is a new series from Christian Alternative focusing upon aspects of Quaker faith and theology. Beginning with *Quaker Roots and Branches* the series will build into a valuable resource both for Quakers and those interested in this unique expression of belief, practice and theology. Watch out for upcoming titles on Quaker theology, faith and practice, and studies in social aspects such as economics and pacifism.

Current other titles...

Quaker Roots and Branches - John Lampen
Telling the Truth About God - Rhiannon Grant

QUAKER QUICKS

What do Quakers Believe?

Geoffrey Durham

CHRISTIAN
ALTERNATIVE

Winchester, UK
Washington, USA

First published by Christian Alternative Books, 2019
Christian Alternative Books is an imprint of John Hunt Publishing Ltd.,
No. 3 East St., Alresford, Hampshire SO24 9EE, UK
office1@jhpbooks.net
www.johnhuntpublishing.com
www.christian-alternative.com

For distributor details and how to order please visit the 'Ordering' section on our website.

Text copyright: Geoffrey Durham 2018

ISBN: 978 1 78535 893 7
978 1 78535 894 4 (ebook)
Library of Congress Control Number: 2018940333

A CIP catalogue record for this book is available from the British Library.

Design: Stuart Davies

Printed and bound by CPI Group (UK) Ltd, Croydon, CR0 4YY, UK
US: Printed and bound by Edwards Brothers Malloy 15200 NBN Way #B, Blue Ridge Summit, PA 17214, USA

Other books by Geoffrey Durham:
The Spirit of the Quakers
Being a Quaker: a guide for newcomers

We operate a distinctive and ethical publishing philosophy in all areas of our business, from our global network of authors to production and worldwide distribution.

Contents

For everyone in the Quaker community at HM Prison, Wayland, UK

Introduction

The seeds of this book were sown during the British general election campaign of 2017. I was watching a TV interview in which a politician was being asked about her plans. She talked, but never answered. For minutes on end she hedged and sloganed and repeated herself and changed the subject, and succeeded in leaving the studio having said nothing, but having said it with elegance and poise. It was a masterpiece of obfuscation.

As my anger subsided, I experienced a moment of terrifying self-awareness. I thought, "I do that. I'm the same. Whenever someone asks me what Quakers believe, I say, 'Well, let me tell you what happened to me,' and I launch into the story of my agnosticism and eventual convincement and, as we shake hands, we agree to talk again. But I've never told her what Quakers believe."

So I decided to write a book answering a reasonable question as reasonably as I can.

It has been a fascinating task. I have published material on this subject in the past, but never quite like this. As before, I have concentrated on the form of Quakerism that I know best, often known as the "non-programmed" tradition; it is widely practised in the UK, Australia, New Zealand, parts of Europe and much of North America. And, as before, I have tried to be objective, so I have referred to Quakers as "they" throughout, despite being one myself. It has served as a useful reminder not to get carried away with my own enthusiasms. But in other ways, this book is different.

Firstly, I have aimed it at the casual enquirer, rather than trying to cater for readers who need to know everything. There are books already available for those who are hungry to know about Quaker structures, or the development of Quaker theology, or the differences in Quaker meetings around the world.

Secondly, I have avoided the specialist jargon that Quakers love. All religious groups develop their own language, but the Quaker version can be particularly hard to grasp, because it uses regular words in irregular ways. So "witness", "worship" and "ministry", for example, have different shades of meaning – and in one or two cases entirely different definitions – from those that a non-Quaker might expect. For that reason I have not featured them, but I have tried not to omit anything that they represent.

Finally, in attempting to answer the title question I have diverged from the usual pattern (start with a description of a silent meeting and move on from there) and have concentrated instead on the shared principles and convictions of Quakers, allowing them to dictate the consequent shape of the book. It has turned my previous thinking on its head and reminded me that Quakers are logical, as well as being passionate and adventurous. They deserve to be more widely understood.

Acknowledgements

As this book was taking shape I accosted just about every Quaker I met in the same way: "Could you tell me what you believe?" I am grateful to them all for their forbearance, but I must thank in particular: Eileen Aird, Anne Charvet, Chaundra Crouch, Val Ferguson, Ingrid Greenhow, Gerald Hewitson, Paula Kingston, John Lampen, Mary Lou Leavitt, Eoin McCarthy, John Reid, Elize Sakamoto, Laura Shipler Chico, Tony Stoller, Imran Tyabji, Chris Venables and Martin Wilkinson.

I owe a great debt to two small groups of Quakers who have allowed me to quote their words. In Chapter 2 they are Alec Davison, Anne Hosking, Jean Jenn, Jennifer Kavanagh and Susan Seymour. For Chapter 8 I recorded conversations with Kelly Burke, Carolyn Hayman, David Henshaw, Maya Metheven, Rajan Naidu, Chloe Scaling, John Shinebourne and Frank Treviss. I am grateful to them all.

Thanks, too, to Alick Beale, from the Communication and Services Department of Quakers in Britain, for permission to quote prolifically from *Quaker Faith & Practice: the book of Christian discipline of the Yearly Meeting of the Religious Society of Friends (Quakers) in Britain* (Fifth edition © 2013, The Yearly Meeting of the Religious Society of Friends [Quakers] in Britain).

And I am deeply grateful as always to my wife, Helen, who has read every word, commented wisely and put up with my endless perplexities. This book could never have been written without her love, understanding and support.

Finally, I want to acknowledge my thanks to the prisoners and Mark Bredin, the Quaker chaplain, at Wayland Prison in Norfolk, UK. They have created a small Quaker community of intense energy and resilience, and have proved, if it needed proving, that Quakerism has the capacity to inspire people with clarity, strength and hope. They have been a wonderful example to me. This book is dedicated to them.

1

The Ways of Quakers

I didn't feel I was "good" enough to be a Quaker. But then I realised that you don't have to be "good" at all. Quakerism is for people who are trying, not people who are succeeding.
Carolyn Hayman

Quakers keep themselves to themselves. It isn't that they are secretive so much as naturally quiet, but the result is the same: no one but a Quaker has a clue who the Quakers are.

Ironically, it's their quietness that many newcomers find most attractive. Quakers don't evangelise. They don't have that fervent desire to convert other people that gives religion a bad name. They don't insist they are right and they never pretend to have all the answers. What they do have is a way of life that, in its detail, is unlike that of any other religious group. And their simple, radical message has a startling modernity that belies its 370-year history.

That message is what this book is about, and I realise it may turn out to be different from what you've already been told. Because Quakers have said so little for so long, there's a good chance that what you've heard has been based on centuries of guesswork, assumptions and misinformation.

At a party the other day, the conversation turned unexpectedly to religion. I said I was a Quaker. One of my fellow guests told me that he thought Quakers were a secret society with funny handshakes. Another asked me why I wasn't wearing a black hat like the smiley old gent on the porridge packet. A third wondered why I was there at all, since Quakers are famous for being puritanical killjoys. All those myths, and many others, need debunking before we can begin.

So I'll tell you what Quakers don't believe, and then I'll explain what they do. Let's begin with the misunderstandings I encountered at the party.

I don't know where the idea of secret handshakes came from and I can't quite believe anyone takes it seriously, but the notion that Quakers are a closed sect – in other words, a religious group who don't encourage newcomers and marry only their own kind – is surprisingly common. Let's set it aside now. Quakers welcome newcomers with open-heartedness and warmth. That means everybody – there isn't a background, eccentricity, nationality or sexual orientation that they ever exclude for any reason. Quakers will regard you as a member of their community as soon as you start to turn up regularly. When it comes to marriage, they labour under no restrictions and marry the person they love, Quaker or not. They were pioneers of same-sex marriage during the early years of the twenty-first century, and their weddings are joyful, uplifting affairs.

On now to the porridge – a much more understandable confusion, since the black-hatted image is still prominent on our supermarket shelves. Quakers have never sold breakfast foods. Not ever. And I'll be astonished if they ever do. The Quaker Oats Company of Chicago (originally from Akron, Ohio) came up with their name in 1877 as a symbol of "good quality and honest value". The firm has no association with any religious group, though their familiar trademark does seem to have been inspired by the figure of William Penn, the British Quaker who travelled to America in 1682 and founded the state of Pennsylvania as a centre of religious tolerance. In his time Quakers wore black and grey, often accompanied by a hat or bonnet. There's no similar convention today, though you may occasionally meet a "plain Quaker"; they wear clothes cut as simply as possible and without conspicuous decoration. Most, however, dress exactly like everyone else, tending to emphasise practicality rather than extravagance.

Their lack of extravagance shouldn't lead you to the conclusion that Quakers don't have any fun. Nor – and I suspect this may be the origin of the idea that they are killjoys – should you associate Quakers with a rejection of the trappings of modern life. Contemporary Quakers live in the world. They are not puritans. They use computers, they go to rock concerts, they drink alcohol, they love art, they shop in the high street, they drive taxis, they eat chocolate, they watch TV.

And while we're about it, let's explode some other common myths that may have confused you. The Quakers are not the Shakers. The Quakers are not the Amish. You don't have to be a vegan to be a Quaker. You don't have to be a vegetarian, either. You can wear lipstick. You don't have to be American. You don't have to be a peace activist. You don't have to believe that every word of the Bible is true.

Too many negatives, I know. But I need to add just one more before the positives can take over. And this is a liberation. In fact, many Quakers ironically find it among the most positive statements they ever make. It's an essential fact about them, and it's a good starting point if you want to know more.

Quakers have no creed.

For many people, particularly religious people, that comes as a shock. How can there be a religious faith with no list of beliefs that its followers have in common? No statement of intent? No dotted line that a person has to sign before they call themselves a Quaker?

There's a one-word answer: experience. Quakers call theirs an experience-based faith. They only believe what they have experienced. They have no truck with dogma. They reject religious doctrine and they don't accept what someone tells them until they've tested it. So being told that "there is a God", or "Jesus died to save us from our sins", or "you will know life after death", cuts no ice with Quakers. As it happens, I know a Quaker who shares all those beliefs, but in each case his conviction comes from an experience he has had. Other Quakers who don't share those experiences won't have reached the same conclusions. Nobody minds.

If you ask a Quaker if she believes in God, you're unlikely to get a quick or easy answer. The first response will probably be, "It depends," and the conversation will meander from there. But since "God" means something different to every human being, it might help you to change the question and explore something that could actually have happened. You could ask, "Have you ever had a spiritual experience you can't explain?" or, "Have you ever felt you were being pushed into doing something by a force you can't control?" or maybe, "Have you ever had an encounter with something you might call God?".

I've never met a Quaker who isn't fascinated by those questions. Quakers have a highly-developed sense of wonder and a constant desire to keep an open mind. They see flashes of the Divine everywhere – in the dancing of a butterfly, or the power of memory, or those fleeting glimpses of the eternal that can catch our inward eye.

And the wonder of revelation is built into Quakers' unique spiritual practice. It is their equivalent of a church service – a communal gathering of anything from two people to about a thousand – and they call it a "meeting". Quaker meetings don't have a formal structure. No two are alike. They are based on silence, stillness, speaking, waiting, listening. As new participants get used to them and their hushed, unpredictable power, Quaker meetings increasingly become a source of spiritual help and a way of finding meaning and purpose.

Between meetings, Quakers keep working on their faith. There's an old Quaker saying they find helpful: *Attend to what love requires of you.* The language may be antiquated, but the sentiment is anything but. It's a call to positive action. It pulls Quakers out of the realm of spiritual wonder and pushes them into the real world. And it's a tough suggestion – it doesn't have the easy convenience of, say, *Attend to what you love* or, still more tempting, *Do what you like*. But behind its toughness lies the combination of kindness and humanity that is a hallmark of Quaker life.

And there are many ways to live it. A large number of Quakers work for peace and social justice, either professionally or in their free time, and they regard the hours they devote to those enterprises as an integral part of their religious lives. Many Quakers pray each day, others never. There are Christian Quakers, Buddhist Quakers, Hindu Quakers. There are huge variations of experience around the role of God in their lives. But, as you might expect from their lack of a creed, the differences and nuances of belief are not seen as obstacles to be overcome. Quakers trust each other to discover for themselves what love requires of them, and to be true to it.

Am I making them sound like saints? I hope not. Quakers are not perfect. They are as flawed, fractious, stubborn and grumpy as anyone else. Like anyone else, they can be thoughtless. Like anyone else, they can be cruel. They know these things about themselves. They reject the idea of sainthood and don't want a reputation for purity.

Their aim is to make sense of the world, to do all they can to mend it, and to live in it peaceably, at the same time helping others to do the same. They have no desire to look good and no patience for the pursuit of moralistic virtue. They are learners in life, not judges of it, and this learning has led them towards some shared understandings and beliefs.

Having started this chapter with a series of Quaker unbeliefs, it seems right to list four basic beliefs that all Quakers seem to me to hold in common:

Quakers believe that formal creeds are unnecessary, because what matters to them is the truth and integrity of personal experience.

Quakers believe that religious doctrines and dogmas are unhelpful and should be set aside.

Quakers believe that regular attendance at Quaker meetings has the power to change people, help them find meaning and give them a purpose in life.

Quakers believe that they should be guided by love and what love requires of them.

It's not an official list – I've based it simply on my own observations. The drawback of writing it down this way, belief after belief after belief, is that you get no sense of the people it describes. I hope to put that right in the chapters that follow, where I'll be saying more about the everyday lives of Quakers, the work they do for peace and social justice, their uniquely transparent ways of reaching business decisions, and the hypnotic magnetism of their meetings.

But I want to focus now on a couple of tiny words from the beginning and end of the list – tiny in size, immense in scope. Quakers talk about them constantly, both separately and as a pair. And they have imbued them with layers of meaning that are seldom recognised by the rest of the world. So, if you want to know more about the ways of Quakers, you need to understand what they mean by love and truth.

Love has the same connotations for Quakers as it has for everyone else – intense affection, sexual drive, warm engagement, passionate involvement. And they are not alone among world religions in extending their loving commitment beyond family and friends to embrace all humanity. Loving others, helping others, finding good in others, even those who have done us harm, can be a tough call, but it's one that Quakers accept with empathy and understanding.

That applies to Quakers' public work in mediation and peacemaking as much as it does to their private lives. It has been the same for centuries. In 1693, when William Penn was making a public case for pacifism, he wrote:

> A good end cannot sanctify evil means; nor must we ever do
> evil, that good may come of it. ... Let us then try what Love
> will do.

And when the eighteenth-century American Quaker John
Woolman sought to build bridges of understanding with the
Native American community of Wyoming, his attitude was the
same:

> Love was the first motion, and thence a concern arose to spend
> some time with the Indians, that I might feel and understand
> their life and the spirit they live in.

We all recognise that "first motion" every day in our family lives
– it's rarer, perhaps, to find the same sentiment holding sway in
the public arena.

As with love, so with truth. All of us can remember lies
we've told – to say nothing of the moments when we've casually
prefixed a sentence with, "to be honest," as if dishonesty
might suddenly emerge as a viable alternative. Quakers are no
different, but they have made up their minds to do what they
can to avoid deceit. Their decision implies straightforwardness,
clarity and a lack of hypocrisy across the board. Quakers once
called themselves "Friends of the Truth" and, while they don't
use that name these days, the use of truth as a one-word mission
statement is still very much alive.

Truth covers so much: a willingness to follow our best
instincts; a reverence for human life; an aspiration to live openly,
honestly and without skeletons in closets; a commitment to
living simply; a respect for the earth; an understanding that the
environment is not ours to destroy.

And truth is political, too: it was a Quaker after all, Milton

Mayer in the 1950s, who first talked about "speaking truth to power".

And what of the pairing? What of love and truth together as a driving force in Quakerism?

For newcomers, a life based on love and truth can sound delightfully refreshing. For seasoned Quakers, that blending of love and truth lies at the root of everything. There is a much-loved Quaker text that begins:

Take heed ... to the promptings of love and truth in your hearts. Trust them as the leadings of God.

A lot of people, I'm sure, will balk at that suggestion. And for all of us it takes some unpacking. It doesn't say, for example, that love, truth and God are the same thing. Nor does it imply that, if you treasure love and truth, you have some kind of hotline to the Almighty.

What it does say is that love and truth are to be found inside us all, and that they can be compared to – perhaps even equated to – what Quakers call *that of God* within us.

And it is such a radical and contentious idea that it deserves a chapter to itself.

2

Inner Light

There have been challenging moments in my life when I've been on the edge of my boundaries and when I've felt supported and held by something that I would call God.
Maya Metheven

Talking about God is risky. It causes clashes, splits and misunderstandings. What counts – and it really is all that counts – is each person's experience of God.

George Fox, one of the first Quakers, gave them a piece of advice in 1656 that they have treasured ever since. He suggested that the actions and behaviour of Quakers could serve as a living example to other people and that, as a result, they would come to "walk cheerfully over the world, answering that of God in every one". Quakers love it and quote it all the time, but that doesn't stop some of them finding its three key words – "that of God" – difficult and obscure. For many, just the word "God" comes tainted with memories of a religious education they would rather forget. So they coin their own phrases to match their experience. I have heard "the Spirit", "the Seed", "the Truth", "God Within", "the Spirit Guide", "the Source", and "the Inward Teacher". One of the most common, as well as being among the oldest – it's been around for at least 370 years – is "the Inner Light".

I've never met anyone – atheist, agnostic, non-theist, all religions, no religion – who doesn't have experience of this Light inside us. We may not talk about it, but we can't deny it. We may not want to look at it, but it's there. It has a lot in common with conscience and with the still, small voice. And it is inextricably bound up with the promptings of love and truth in our hearts.

Whatever words Quakers use to express this Inner Light, it

is a reality for them. They often talk about it pushing or moving them. It guides them. They feel it.

Some of my Quaker friends have allowed me to quote snatches of their experience:

Light is probably the word I use most of all.

I cannot escape from the embrace of the Spirit within me and all around me.

In my life experience, the Divine has been a reality.

I experience God as the life-force.

Truth for me is the personal encounter with the Divine.

I can live with the term God as energy, force, direction, rather than a thing or a person.

I have had experiences that I can only attribute to the presence of a power beyond myself – an energy quickened by love and truth – which I access without an intermediary.

These quotations originated separately from one another; they were never part of one conversation. What strikes me about them is just how much each of the speakers has in common with the others, and how much of their language is identical: "experience", "energy", "force". These Quakers may not have a formal creed to fall back on, but they share such a wealth of understanding, insight and yes, belief, that in the end it makes little difference.

These people are describing the everyday spirituality of their ordinary lives. Nothing in their statements represents a doctrine they have been taught, or a dogma someone has told them to believe. And it's significant, I think, that two of them talk about encountering an Outer Light as well as an Inner one. The first person talks of the "Spirit within me and all around me"; the other of "a power beyond myself".

I've gained a strong impression over the years that many Quakers – dare I say most of them? – share this experience of a guiding spirit that moves and inspires them from the outside as it enlivens and pushes them within. For these Quakers, the Inner and the Outer Light have become one. The Spirit is within them and it is all around. And their religious practice as Quakers helps them to maintain their relationship with the Divine.

The last person I've quoted adds something significant. He says there is a "power beyond myself ... which I access *without an intermediary*". In other words, to put it in terms that, say, a Christian might use, he doesn't need a priest to help him encounter the energy he experiences, because he has discovered that it is possible for him to reach it directly through his own practice as a Quaker. He has no need of a go-between.

This is a principle that has got Quakers into serious trouble with religious authorities over the years. They don't need priests or trained holy people to interpret their religion for them, because they are all the priests. Their communities are carefully structured to eliminate any form of hierarchy – I'll explain that more fully later – and to run smoothly with nobody in charge. It would be tempting to call this self-government, but it really isn't: Quakers are powered by the energy they discover inside and beyond them, and their communities function in the same way.

Words can fail us. "Within" and "beyond" are not adequate to express the mystical connection that lies at the heart of Quaker life. It goes deeper than words. Each Quaker expresses it in a different way. What is incontrovertible is the vigour and clarity that they all experience through their unmediated relationship with the Divine. It has led to a refusal to accept any kind of religious theory and a rejection of the traditional trappings of religious authority.

Those attitudes shine a light on some core Quaker beliefs. There is no hierarchy, because Quakers believe that we are all equal. And I don't mean just Quakers, I mean everybody. Each of us, as they often say, is "unique, precious, a child of God".

Quakers believe in the absolute equality of everyone on the planet. They don't accept distinctions of any kind.

That's not to say that they don't accept distinctiveness, they do. They enjoy eccentricity and peculiarity and quirk. Equality is not sameness. It is understanding that we are all of equal worth. It is treating everyone with equal respect, regardless of age, sexual orientation, background, ethnicity or upbringing: the ultimate expression of love and truth. Children must be given the same respect as adults; their views must be sought and acted upon. The poor and destitute must be valued as warmly as those lucky enough to have work. The uniqueness and preciousness of each individual must be treasured.

Every day, too, is special. Every day is holy. No day is better, more noteworthy or more important than any other, because every day is sacred. Quakers don't have what some religious groups call a "church calendar", marking this day as significant and that one as ordinary. They can commemorate the births, deaths, sadnesses and joys of their religion – to say nothing of their own personal lives – on any or every day they choose. They don't feel the need for a predetermined rota.

And so it follows, doesn't it, that Quakers have no Sabbath. They hold their meetings on any day that is convenient. For practical reasons that is often Sunday, because it's a day when many people have free time, but Sunday is no more holy or special for them than any other day. Today is the Sabbath, because it's the Sabbath every day.

It also means that Quakers don't celebrate religious festivals – at least they don't celebrate them as specifically religious. So while they will want to be with family and friends having a good time at, say, Christmas or Chanukah, they won't set aside the day as one of particular spiritual significance.

Quakers make no distinction between the sacred and the secular in any aspect of their lives. This is a religion of the everyday. So Quakers don't have any specially consecrated ground or particularly holy places, because every place is holy for Quakers.

Newcomers to the Quaker way who have no religious background often find these beliefs refreshing – indeed, many find them beautiful. They can be harder to grasp for those who have been brought up with a faith that insists on sainthood, or distinctions between one person and another, or a particular brand of holiness. Such people can understandably find the next step in Quaker belief hard to grasp, as well – it can seem too great a leap in the thought process, too much to take in – but it has a fullness and scope that many find endlessly engaging.

Quakers believe that they should live sacramentally.

"Sacramental" is a not a common word. I'm trying to avoid Quaker jargon in this book – and I'm only allowing myself "sacramental" on the grounds that it's a borderline case – but the fact is that I can't find another one that fits. My dictionary defines "sacrament" as "an outward and visible sign of an inward divine grace". Living sacramentally means allowing that grace to flow through us. It means acknowledging that all of life is holy and daring ourselves to behave accordingly. It reminds us that we don't own the world, that we can behave unselfishly, that we can show loving consideration for all creatures, and that we can live simply, working for a more peaceful world.

People who have grown up in a Christian tradition sometimes assume the Quaker meaning of "sacrament" is the same as theirs. Their communion service, or Eucharist, is a sacrament and so they deduce that for Quakers, who have no such ritual, all meals must consequently be sacramental in the same way. That is certainly true for some, but it's by no means the case for every Quaker. And it's a narrow view: for Quakers, sacramental living is a joyful affirmation of the riches the world has to offer, together with an acknowledgement – a crucial one – that there is much that needs mending. Quakers gladly embrace it all. They regard helping others as part of life, as their way of being in the world.

That brings me back to the sentence of George Fox's that I quoted a few pages ago: "Walk cheerfully over the world, answering that of God in every one." Some Quakers have expressed surprise that I'm not inclined to list it as one of the core Quaker beliefs. It certainly appears in many books and websites that introduce Quakerism to newcomers. "Quakers believe," they say, "that there is that of God in everyone." I understand and respect that.

But it seems to me that, by expressing it that way, they miss the crux of what George Fox was saying. His objective was not to persuade Quakers to believe in a God within, but to encourage them to take action. He assumed that we all have "that of God" inside us and exhorted Quakers to answer it in other people.

He knew that, for him, God was a reality. He was suggesting that Quakers should spend their lives seeking out that reality in the hearts of other people. He looked for the goodness in everyone. He knew it was there, because goodness is a reality too, so he dedicated his life to finding it in each person he met. That didn't just mean colleagues, friends and family. It meant enemies, criminals, the wicked, the cruel, the depraved. And today, Quakers still believe in the reality of goodness. And they believe in doing all they can to find it.

That means having a respect for others and being prepared to try to find the natural goodness they were born with, even when it has been corrupted and flattened by the cruelty of the times. That is why Quakers have always been willing to engage with prisoners serving life sentences, for example; they may hate the crime, but they will do all they can not to hate the criminal. They know from their experience that finding love and truth in everyone may not be as joyous as it sounds. It can be a laborious, uphill climb.

Let's draw together some of these beliefs, all of which come as a direct result of the life experience of Quakers:

Quakers believe that there is an energy, a power of love

and truth within and beyond us, that pushes us towards what is good and is accessible to everyone without an intermediary.

Quakers believe in the reality of goodness.

Quakers believe that each one of us is unique, precious, a child of God.

Quakers believe that every person, every place, every day is holy.

Quakers believe that all of life is sacramental.

I'm aware that, without a context, this is just a collection of worthy thoughts. What turns them into a way of life is the power Quakers derive from their meetings. Quaker meetings are the absolute bedrock of the Quaker faith. They can change people.

In the next chapter, I'll explain how they work, why many people find they can't keep away for long, and what it is about this hour of near-silence that helps Quakers in their ambition to seek out the Inner Light in everyone.

3

Quaker Meetings

I enjoy Quaker meetings. I really enjoy them. I have to go.
Frank Treviss

At that party, the one I mentioned a few pages ago, a guest told me what a Quaker meeting was. "I know what they do." he said. "They sit around in silence and every so often someone says something."

He wasn't totally mistaken. But, by observing the spiritual practice of Quakers casually, at a distance, through the wrong end of a telescope, he missed most of its essence and all of its power. A Quaker meeting is greater than the sum of its parts. It can be a revelation to people looking for meaning and purpose in their lives.

It is called by a number of names, but none that hints at what's really going on. It is often referred to as a "meeting for worship", but that confuses more people than it helps. Some people call it a "silent meeting", but that's misleading. "Still" might be better, or even "tranquil", but no adjective quite hits the spot. So, in the absence of anything better, I'm going for the most self-explanatory: Quaker meeting. It's the simplest, too.

Quaker meetings are hard to pin down, because no two are the same. They are unpredictable. There's no structure, no set form of words, no one deciding what happens next. They stand or fall by their impact on each participant, yet they are possibly the most communal, mutual, *shared* religious events that anyone can experience.

And they are adventurous: no one goes into a Quaker meeting knowing the outcome; they can comfort, they can discomfort, they can surprise. You might turn up for weeks without feeling much benefit and then, out of the blue, attend one that fills you with rhapsodic delight. Quaker meetings have been life-changing for some people, while providing others with a constant, reliable backbone, a spiritual basis from which they can take decisions and discover what they want to do in the world. Quaker meetings serve many functions and they work in many ways.

If you have reason to feel grateful for your life you may be looking for a space in which to offer thanks. A Quaker meeting gives you the stillness you need. If you feel sorrow you may need a space to grieve. You'll find it in a Quaker meeting. You can express personal joys and explore spiritual turning points. Help can be found. Truths can be faced. Quaker meetings allow the Divine to teach and transform you.

All of which, I realise, sounds inflated and unrealistic to anyone who hasn't tried them. So if you're at all interested, perhaps you could make the experiment? You could go, learn how they work, attend them for a few weeks, try taking part. You might discover from your own experience, as thousands have before you, that meetings have the power to change people and show them new ways of living. And then again you might not. The whole thing might leave you cold. But at least you'll know.

So what are Quaker meetings? I'll explain the basics and add a little advice as I go, in case you decide to give one a try.

They can happen anywhere – community centres, living rooms, prisons, hospital wards, even the open air. You just need an area in which people can sit comfortably in a circle. The only place you can't hold a Quaker meeting is at home on your own – unless you try one of the growing number of online meetings.

Most meetings are held in Quaker "meeting houses", which are designed to accommodate not only the local Quakers, but also a host of community activities: yoga classes, nursery schools, ballet lessons, Alcoholics Anonymous, choirs, drama groups, mindfulness courses, and a lot more besides.

Let's assume you've decided to try a Quaker meeting in one of these meeting houses. You'll find a room laid out with chairs or benches. They will probably be in rows, but it's unlikely that the seating will only face one way. In almost all cases it will be laid out in a circle or a square, or any other pattern that allows everyone to see everyone else.

In the middle of the room there may be a table. It is important to understand that this is not an altar. It is just a central point, provided simply for the convenience of everyone present. It may have flowers on it, a jug of water and glasses, and a few key books for people to consult if they need to.

The meeting begins when the first person walks into the room. Little by little, others come in and sit down. They may acknowledge the presence of friends with a smile, but they don't speak, because it's important for everyone to stay silent as a meeting starts to get under way. As they gather themselves for the time ahead, the participants are beginning a process through which they calm themselves and surrender to the silence.

Everyone starts in their own way. There are no rules. If there are people you know in the room, you might want to acknowledge their presence to yourself – a Quaker meeting, after all, is communal. You might want to sit with your eyes closed, or with them open. You might find it helps to place your hands on your knees, or have them resting gently in your lap, or hanging loosely by your side. Keeping your feet planted on the floor, legs slightly apart, works for some people. Nobody minds. Treat it all as an experiment.

You may find it hard to clear your head. Unpaid bills, school reports, family upheavals, workplace disputes vie for your attention and refuse to give way. As the silence gathers, all the worries of the week jostle and yammer in your brain.

Everybody develops their own techniques for handling this brain-babble and most agree that it gets easier. What doesn't work for anyone is to pretend it isn't happening. A lot of people find the best strategy is to acknowledge the presence of their demon chatterer and simply set it to one side: "Thank you, I'll deal with you later." Then, for a few minutes, the tranquil self has an opportunity to flourish. With practice, those minutes increase in number to thirty, forty, even sixty minutes of refreshing, welcoming quiet. And it can be surprising to discover, after a month or two of going regularly to meetings, that a whole hour of silence feels curiously short.

So what do you think about as you start this process? A personal mantra can help. One person I know says the words of an ancient psalm in her head: "Be still and know that I am God." She repeats them slowly to herself, missing each final word or two as she goes, until she is breathing a single "be" to her semiconscious mind.

Another person has a way of silently expressing his gratefulness for his life. As he gives thanks he is able to see himself and others with a kindness and humility that he isn't always able to find. He gives way to a better self inside him.

Whatever techniques the participants in a meeting are using to help themselves, this little knot of people is slowly becoming connected one to another. As they surrender to the peace, the atmosphere gradually changes. The tranquillity becomes deeper, the serenity more profound. There's no silence like a Quaker silence. It becomes part of you. As it grows in intensity, you can almost touch it.

For some people who haven't ever attended a Quaker meeting, just the thought of this prolonged silence is mildly terrifying. They don't believe that an hour of it can possibly feel right, so they worry that they'll be in for sixty minutes of nothingness. And it's understandable. Their experience of life tells them that silence means something has gone wrong: they've forgotten the name of the person they're talking to, or they find themselves suddenly lost for words, or they're staring at the floor in tongue-tied embarrassment. So they associate silence with emptiness, discomfort, and the muffled shame of having nothing to say.

But a Quaker meeting isn't a vacuum, it's full. And a Quaker silence isn't sudden, it's planned. Nor is this simply a "silent meeting", despite the tendency of many people to call it that, because it's anything but soundless. There's so much to be used and absorbed: the gentle whimper of a baby perhaps, or the shuffling of shoes on a wooden floor, or the rumble of buses in the street outside. The silence of Quakers is just a tool, an aid to achieving what their meetings are really striving for – and that is a nurturing stillness.

When a Quaker meeting has been in progress for a while it sometimes happens that the participants begin to find themselves enveloped in something new: an all-embracing canopy of peace and warmth. The quiet centre of each individual has become a mutual centre for everyone. The communal silence has melded the participants to one another, giving way to a tranquillity that gathers around them and covers the room. The meeting has become truly still.

In the stillness people find that a life of the spirit becomes possible. Some people use the word "God" for the force they encounter now, still more "the Light", others talk just of "something other", but all agree that they are in touch with an insistent energy that takes them over. It often happens that their hearts beat louder and faster. They may find themselves able to give attention to the Light inside them.

At these times – often just a few precious seconds – people are able to take stock of their lives and see the truth of themselves full on, without the need to present a face to the world. They may experience fresh insights. Their serenity may give way to new-found mental clarity. They may be able to take decisions, initiate crucial changes, or see friends and family from a different perspective. At the very least, these moments constitute a welcome reality check. At best, they are imbued with the bliss of self-discovery.

Silence is not the only aid to the nurturing stillness of a Quaker meeting. There is another – and that, ironically, seems in many ways to be its opposite. It is speech.

It happens from time to time that a member of the group feels a sudden prompting to say something out loud that they hadn't expected to voice at all. This need to speak will always be involuntary. When someone feels it, they weigh it up in their mind and decide whether this is a message for them or for the group as a whole. If it's something that seems relevant only to their own life, they keep quiet and let it work in their mind. But if it needs to be spoken to everyone, they stand and say it out into the stillness, as briefly and succinctly as they can.

It isn't necessarily an easy process and it's important to bear in mind that ego should never be a factor in it. The rest of the group is not an audience to be impressed. The speaker is not a guru. This isn't group therapy or a discussion. And it certainly isn't a debate. Speakers don't speak more than once and it's the custom for everyone to stay silent for a while after they've sat down, so that what they've said can be fully taken in and understood.

Sometimes more than one person will stand to speak during the course of a meeting. As a result, a strand may emerge and turn into a theme that everyone becomes engaged with. Or just as common is the meeting in which the spoken contributions appear unrelated to one another until a connection suddenly reveals itself during the last few minutes. And there are meetings in which nothing is said. They can sometimes be the deepest of all.

Most meetings last about an hour. When the time comes to finish, two people who have been appointed to close the proceedings quietly shake hands with each other. Their cue is picked up by everyone and the whole meeting becomes wreathed in smiles as the participants shake hands with those sitting nearest to them. It's a happy custom.

There are one or two recommendations worth mentioning, but no rules. First, a piece of advice: it's not a good idea to be late. I'm sure you'll have understood why by now: this is a communal practice, so a steady stream of latecomers changes the make-up of the community with each arrival. If everyone is on time, they can see who's there from the beginning.

And a suggestion: if you want to ruin a Quaker meeting – and I hope you don't – there are two surefire ways to go about it. The first is to go in knowing that you've prepared something good to say and that you're planning to say it. The second is to go in knowing that you aren't going to say anything at all. In both cases, you're destroying the spiritual spontaneity of the occasion. The more you're tempted to control, the less you'll gain.

The unpredictability of Quaker meetings ensures that everyone responds to them in their own way. So, as we reach the end of this chapter, I'm going to make some observations about the consequences of Quaker meetings, rather than listing any beliefs:

In their meetings, Quakers allow the Divine to teach and transform them.

Quakers find it possible to connect with their emotions, see their lives in perspective, and address personal difficulties through the power of Quaker meetings.

Quakers have found it possible to have life-transforming spiritual encounters in Quaker meetings.

Quakers have experiences in their meetings that inspire them to take action in the world.

The reality check, self-discovery and moments of enlightenment that can be part of a Quaker meeting sometimes lead the participants to make changes in their lives. Those changes, and the action that can ensue, form the next chapter of the story.

4

One Thing Leads to Another

*Enlightenment is just around the corner, but you've got to be quick
to spot it. If you're not careful you can turn round and find the
light's gone out.*
David Henshaw

When they sit in meetings, Quakers often call it "waiting". They
have a number of ways of expressing the same thing. Some talk
about "waiting on God", others "expectant waiting". Still more
say they are "waiting in the Light".

What are they waiting for? It isn't the same for everyone
and, even it were, it wouldn't be easy to express clearly. I know
Quakers who describe it as waiting to be told something, but
they don't hear mysterious voices. Others wait for guidance, but
they don't believe in a master plan. What Quakers experience,
I think, as they wait in the stillness, are moments of personal
recognition and enlightenment.

There may also be moments of sudden reversal, of course, or
of dazzling inspiration, but for most people the process involves
a slow uncovering of truths that have always been there but have
lain in their hearts unnoticed, like familiar images that take on
fresh slants by being lit in new and unexpected ways.

Often the image will be an aspect of a person's work or home
life that becomes clearer simply by being seen in a different
light. Or, viewing things with fresh eyes, a person may perceive
a niggling sense of public injustice that forces them to speak out
and take action. Sometimes it will be something unrecognised by
government or ignored by the world; frequently it will acquire
intense significance for the person who has uncovered it.

In 1919 the Quaker William Braithwaite wrote:

Evils which have struck their roots deep in the fabric of human society are often accepted, even by the best minds, as part of the providential ordering of life. They lurk unsuspected in the system of things.

From their beginnings in the mid-seventeenth century, Quakers have made it their business to expose the anomalies they regard as injustices and do all they can to put an end to them. They have regularly found themselves in opposition to the spirit of the age, as it fails to notice the evils lurking "in the system of things".

From the start, Quakers' perception that each person is unique and precious was regarded as bizarre by the rest of the world. Quakers always insisted that men were the equals of women, that differences of religious faith caused unnatural divisions, that each person was deserving of respect. Equality was one of the many principles of the Quaker pioneers that kept landing them in prison.

A hundred years later they were among the first to discern that slavery was an evil that had to be eradicated. They were met with fierce opposition. It was another century-and-a-half before slavery was abolished.

And those two evils, inequality and the slave trade, still lurk unsuspected in the systems of things, centuries after those early Quakers combated them. Quakers today emulate their ancestors in fighting them at every possible opportunity. They march, they form pressure groups, they expose the wicked and the underhand, they work behind the scenes to effect change.

Quakers' belief in equality is a bedrock of their faith. The world pays lip service to the notion of equality without caring to explore its depth and range. Quakers campaign for prison reform, the rights of young people to vote, the rights of prisoners to vote, the rights of children, the rights of the disabled, the rights of asylum seekers, the rights of gay, lesbian, bisexual, transgender and intersex people. They reject ageism in all its forms. All that matters is the multiplicity of gifts each person brings. Age is no guarantee either of fitness or of wisdom.

Quakers oppose the treatment of any human being as "other". In times of war, the enemy is always other, because it's so much easier to kill people with whom you have no connection. So they are demonised: they become Huns, Nips, Gooks, Haji. And in peacetime any number of groups – the poor, the young, the homeless, the Jewish, the Muslim, the Romany, the American, the un-American – are regarded as other. Yet we know in our hearts that there is no other. We are one. We share a common humanity.

If there were true equality in every aspect of life, the world would be transformed. It is a transformation that Quakers long for. Any inequality among people is offensive to them. They oppose all forms of hierarchy and do all they can to eliminate it in their own affairs. Their whole religion and entire way of life stem from their devotion to equality and their desire to give equal respect to all people. Society sees these as social issues, and they are political too, but for Quakers inequality is a religious matter. They regard it as a fundamental wickedness.

One thing leads to another. No one changes overnight, but once people start thinking about equal rights their perceptions of the world begin to alter. They notice sink-holes in every path they tread: double standards of justice, double standards of truth, double standards everywhere.

One particular double standard that has resonance for Quakers takes place daily in our courts. If you are called to give evidence you are asked to swear that you will tell the truth. In the act of delivering the oath you are implicitly admitting that, although you won't lie for the next few minutes, you might have lied yesterday and you reserve the right to lie tomorrow. So today becomes a special case. As a favour to the court, you are promising not to start lying until the judge says you are free to leave.

For three-and-a-half centuries, Quakers have rejected the entire scenario. They refuse to swear oaths at any time.

Their devotion to truth doesn't just involve not lying. A double standard might mean, for example, turning a blind eye to an unethical practice that I know my employer has decided to pursue. Or, at an everyday level, not pointing out a simple mistake when a store assistant gives me too much change. The passion of Quakers for equality and truth involves a daily multitude of tiny, insignificant decisions that add up to a way of life.

"True" means "trusted". It also means "real". And so a pursuit of truth becomes a constant scenario in which Quakers strive for integrity – and, with that, honesty, sincerity and straightforwardness. And, with those, a desire to speak plainly, an inclination to acknowledge mistakes and a willingness to apologise appropriately. One thing keeps leading to another.

Worthy ambitions of this kind are often seen by the world as dull, stodgy and bland. That's because the world has never tried them for long enough to experience the calm, balance and tranquillity of mind they produce. Quakers are not killjoys – many people are surprised by their exuberance – and they know that joy can appear from unexpected sources.

One of those sources is the impulse to live a simple life. It's more than a desire to avoid extravagance (though that comes into it) and isn't just about getting rid of clutter (though that's part of it too). It's an expression of Quakers' need to clear out the obstacles that stand in the way of their connection to other human beings. Many Quakers don't stop there. They say that, for them, simplicity means trying to remove everything that blocks them from God.

Its most obvious manifestation is in Quaker meetings themselves: no symbols, no crosses, no stars, no stained glass. Just the power of silence and stillness in a plain, undecorated room. The experience of Quakers is that the devotional aids that some religious groups use – statues, for example, or painted images, or beautifully embroidered cloths – get in the way of their unmediated relationship with the Divine. Emblems of that kind are intended to help with the life of the spirit. Quakers don't deny their beauty and they may adore them as works of art, but they rarely experience them as useful in their religious lives.

They aren't inspired by emblems in other aspects of their lives, either. I have never, for example, known a Quaker to have any interest in designer labels or luxury goods, because they aren't attracted to the idea of becoming members of some imaginary consumerist elite. Which is not to say that they are drawn to the cheap or the shoddy. There is an old Quaker advice to "choose what is simple and beautiful" and Quakers like to stand by it.

They often quote Gandhi's dictum, "Live simply, that others may simply live", one of many sayings of the Indian leader that they hold dear. And they love the memory of the man himself, too, for the simplicity of his lifestyle and his belief in non-violence as a pathway to radical change. He maintained a strong relationship with Quakers all his life, choosing the meeting house in London's Euston Road for his first public speech in the capital in 1931, and visiting Woodbrooke Quaker Study Centre in Birmingham, where he spoke on his ambition to achieve freedom through peaceful means.

Quakers share that ambition today. They give what they can to help casualties of war, refugees, victims of totalitarianism. Some travel to war-ravaged nations to offer assistance. They are supported by their communities, by their national bodies, and by the permanent offices at the United Nations in Geneva and New York known as QUNO, where Quakers provide facilities for UN diplomats, staff, and non-governmental partners to work on difficult issues in a quiet atmosphere out of the public eye.

One significant ingredient of a simple life is the principle of "a fair day's work for a fair day's pay", so it follows that dreams of a fast buck or a win on the horses don't cause Quaker hearts to beat faster. And it is exactly that dreaming, that fantasy, that opportunity to lose oneself – literally – in the unrealistic pursuit of sudden wealth, that sets them so firmly against the gambling industry.

And I realise that this is sounding implausibly high-minded, so once again I have to be clear that Quakers have fun. The image of the severe, finger-wagging, black-hatted Quaker is entirely misplaced. They party and enjoy it, dance and enjoy it, celebrate, laugh and sing, and enjoy it all. They are simply aware that enjoyments stop being enjoyments when they take over our lives.

They don't set the bar impossibly high. They never make rules for themselves or impose requirements. It's noticeable, though, that, without any stipulations or enforced guidance, newcomers often begin to make life changes as they start to attend meetings regularly. It's a slow process, both conscious and unconscious, but many look for ways to alter their behaviour and modify their attitudes. There's never any persuasion. Quakers don't proselytise or indoctrinate. It is the stillness that does it, the stillness and the waiting, and the uncovering of what's inside.

There's a centuries-old suggestion that helps. Quakers call it "as long as you can". If you want to make changes in your life, they suggest that you continue to live in the old way without a thought for the new, until you begin slowly to embarrass yourself. Your better judgement makes you feel uneasy. You realise that it's going to be simpler – not more virtuous, just simpler – to stop the old behaviour than continue with it.

If there's a habit you want to lose – chocolate, say, or caffeine, or driving the kids to school when you could walk – you talk to your friends and family about it and tell them what you would like to do, but you don't necessarily stop. You just continue with it *as long as you can*. And after a while you gradually notice that you are losing the desire for chocolate, or caffeine, or driving around the corner. You've reached the point at which you *can't*. It's a good Quaker principle, because (a) it works, and because (b) we all need gentle and kindly ways of learning to live differently.

It's time to list some more of these beliefs, attitudes and impulses that shape the Quaker way of life:

> **Equality, truth and simplicity are essential elements of the Quaker way.**
>
> **Quakers believe that we are all one, sharing a common humanity: no person is less deserving of respect than any other.**
>
> **Quakers honour loving, non-exploitative relationships, irrespective of gender or sexual orientation.**
>
> **Quakers try to live simply; they believe that a simple life freely chosen is a source of strength.**
>
> **Quakers believe that any deep-rooted custom of society, however commonplace or entrenched, should be opposed if it is unjust.**
>
> **Quakers believe from their experience that honesty and integrity bring freedom to the mind and joy to the spirit.**
>
> **Quakers reject double standards of truth and so avoid swearing oaths; instead, they are content to affirm.**
>
> **Quakers are wary of behaviours and substances that can become addictive.**

It's time, too, to repeat one that I mentioned a few pages ago. It's so integral to this chapter and the next that it seems right to quote it again now.

> **Quakers believe that every person, every place, every day is holy.**

If everything that lives is holy, it must be wrong to kill it. That belief dominates Quakers' attitudes, both to caring for the planet and to preparing for war. It is to those issues that I want to turn next.

5

Everything That Lives Is Holy

Simplicity, truth, equality and peace: therefore sustainability.
Kelly Burke

Quakers have always been campaigners. In the mid to late 1600s they fought for the right to hold their meetings and were pursued and persecuted by the authorities, finding themselves at odds with the views of the majority. Many of those pioneering Quakers were imprisoned and tortured for their beliefs.

Two-and-a-half centuries later they clashed with mainstream society again, when around two-thirds of the young British Quakers who were conscripted to serve in the First World War declined to fight for reasons of conscience. Some were sent to prison, others sentenced to hard labour and those who were compelled to fight did so in the knowledge that, if they refused to obey orders, they would almost certainly be shot.

A spirit of protest remains part of the Quaker character today. They still regularly find themselves out on a limb, at variance with the spirit of the age, campaigning for sustainability, equal rights and social justice. And they maintain an uncompromising position on all forms of aggressive violence.

There's a line from a 1793 poem by William Blake, *America: a prophecy*, that epitomises the Quaker way:

For every thing that lives is holy, life delights in life.

Blake was not a Quaker, but what he wrote tunes in perfectly with Quakers' religious instincts: that the whole of life is sacramental; that we share a common humanity; that no person is less deserving of respect than any other; and, most fundamental of all, that we should not respond with violence to our fellow human beings.

How innocent and unworldly those instincts sound! And how unlike the teachings of some of the world's most familiar belief systems.

Take the Ten Commandments for example, and in this case particularly the sixth: *Thou shalt not kill*. Almost as soon as it was written "with the finger of God" that principle acquired a curious, unaccountable flexibility. Religious leaders explained that, on this occasion, God didn't really know what he was talking about. "It's not supposed to be taken literally." "It depends on the circumstances." "It just means murder; killing and murder are not the same thing."

So governments of Christian countries still justify the bombing of foreign cities, religious leaders rejoice at military victories and reasonable people defend wars they regard as "just".

Quakers approach these matters differently. They believe that war is always an admission of failure. They believe that *Thou shalt not kill* means what it says. And they make a clear distinction between, on the one hand, a just cause and, on the other, a just war.

There are many just causes – we all know dozens – but most Quakers believe there is no such thing as a just war. Just causes should be addressed in every legitimate way possible: the deployment of peacebuilding initiatives before a flashpoint is reached; the use of intermediaries; formal diplomacy; non-formal diplomacy. Quakers have a long history of involvement in such activities. They do not regard mass murder as a useful solution to the problems of the world.

How have they arrived at views so different from those of some other religious groups? You know the answer, but it can bear repetition: they wait in the stillness of their meetings, they contemplate the Inner Light in people, and they know in the quiet of their hearts that they can never murder another human being or allow another human to be murdered in their name.

They appreciate the sincerity of those who believe that wars can be just. All hostilities begin with a humanitarian motive: this dictator must be stopped, or that act of aggression must be punished. But problems begin to overwhelm good intentions as soon as the cruelty begins. The outcome of a conflict is always out of the control of those who participate in it. War creates hardship and suffering and causes new crises as it gradually becomes clear that, while one form of tyranny may have been contained, another is poised to take its place. However well an act of war is planned it spins out of control, engendering new difficulties and ushering in more horrors.

It doesn't need to be that way. Regime change in South Africa during the early 1990s, widely predicted to become a bloodbath, was achieved peacefully through painstaking negotiation. And we can all quote other examples of peaceful settlements of conflict, because the crucial fact often ignored is that peacemaking can be learnt. It can be taught. It is complex and difficult, but no more so than war. If governments spent more money on techniques for creating peace before war can begin, and correspondingly less on weapons of devastation and misery, we would live in a saner world.

Quakers today are active in peacebuilding, attempting to reconcile warring factions and mediating between them, often working on the ground with the sound of bombing and gunfire ringing in their ears.

They campaign on both sides of the Atlantic for the peacetime rights of conscientious objectors. The National Campaign for a Peace Tax Fund in the USA and Conscience in the UK are active in campaigning for the rights of citizens to divert the portion of their tax currently spent on war to peacebuilding and conflict-prevention. Both organisations have a significant Quaker presence.

Again, it was a group of Quakers who began the world's first

Alternatives to Violence Project at Green Haven Prison in New York, helping to develop participants' abilities to resolve conflicts without resorting to manipulation, coercion or violence. AVP International has now spread to fifty countries and is staffed almost entirely by volunteers.

In the UK Quakers founded Leap Confronting Conflict, an organisation that supports young people to make changes in their lives by gaining a greater understanding of themselves and their relationship with conflict.

It doesn't have to be a Quaker initiative for Quakers to become involved. For example, when they heard about Circles of Support and Accountability, started in Canada by the Mennonites, Quakers recognised the value of the project and became involved. The Circles help convicted sex offenders to resettle after their release from prison, in order to reduce the possibility of their offending again. Groups of, say, five volunteers meet regularly with the offender who is the central member of the Circle. Advice can be given on housing, employment, money and the other vital issues that confront anyone who is released from prison. All the emphasis is on inclusion rather than exclusion, both in the context of the Circles and in society as a whole. Survivors of sexual offending are not forgotten, either: a top priority of this work is that there should be no more victims. It's active mediation of a kind that Quakers are particularly drawn to.

I could fill the rest of this book with details of Quaker initiatives that help people to learn techniques for mediation, peacebuilding and conflict resoluton, but there's more to say about Quakers than that and I'm aware that I might not be giving a true picture. Many of them are grateful for such enterprises without playing a major part in them. They have regular jobs, live conventional lives and support peacemaking projects whenever they can.

And, like most people, they don't agree with each other all the time. Positions on peace, in particular, vary from Quaker to Quaker. They often talk things over among themselves, and many of them find that explaining the ways of Quakers to newcomers helps to clarify their own views on subjects that are never simple or clear-cut.

People often ask if they would prohibit all uses of force. Most Quakers, I think, would say no. They accept that a creative deployment of force can frequently be necessary in restraining someone intent on doing harm. What they reject is the idea that destructive, violent aggression solves problems.

And they are often asked a popular hypothetical question to which there really is only one answer.

"What would you do if an intruder was attacking your mother?"

"Well, help her, of course."

People often assume that you have to be a pacifist to be a Quaker. Absolutely not. Quakerism is an experience-based faith, so it's your experience that matters; and if that hasn't led you to a particular position on peace, or war, or armaments, or conflict resolution, no Quaker is going to try to persuade you. It may be that you have experiences to share of success achieved through armed peace-keeping. Nobody objects to that, either. Quakers don't regard pacifism as the answer to everything.

And they rarely describe themselves as "pacifists". There's something about the word that doesn't quite work for them. Perhaps it's just the first two syllables. That word inside the word – "passive" – makes them sound as if they are in favour of lying on the ground with their legs in the air or curling up into a ball until the nasty people go away. That doesn't describe Quakers. They aren't passivists. They're activists.

But their activism is frequently not the stuff of headlines. It begins with themselves: at home, at work, at school, in their daily lives. They try to live peaceably, treat everyone with respect and avoid making prejudiced judgements about the lives of others. They look carefully at their behaviour and make changes where they can. But, like anyone else, Quakers are entirely capable of acting in ways which lead to aggression and offence.

We have all experienced the difference between anger (a natural feeling experienced by everyone) and rage (a dangerous distortion of the same emotion). We all know what it is to suffer from envy, malice and spite. We are all, to a greater or lesser extent, intrigued by power. We like to win. We can find it hard learning how to lose. Quakers try to search out the elements in their lives, like these, that contain what they call "the seeds of war".

There's a saying, widely attributed to Gandhi but probably coined by the Quaker A. J. Muste, that they find useful:

There is no way to peace. Peace is the way.

In other words, just do it. Do it now. But don't do it in the hope of attaining some long-term, unattainable goal. Do it in the hundreds of tiny, apparently insignificant ways that accumulate to make a difference. Make it a way of life.

And they have exactly the same attitude to another struggle that threatens to kill us all: the global emergency caused by climate change. Care of the planet has become an urgent issue for Quakers, embracing many of the concerns that have preoccupied them for centuries: the equality of all people, the importance of living for the truth of every situation, a care for the earth, a striving for simplicity and an understanding that all of life is sacramental.

They were early to spot it. In 1772 John Woolman wrote:

To impoverish the earth now to support outward greatness appears to be an injury to the succeeding age.

They were relatively late to appreciate the catastrophe that it has become. In the twenty-first century, however, it has become a slowly-developing passion for them. Aware that they have unknowingly contributed just as much to global warming as anyone else, they have resolved to change themselves.

Here is Gandhi again:

> If we could change ourselves, the tendencies in the world would also change.

Quakers are attempting, as far as they can, to become a low-carbon community, cutting down on their greenhouse gas emissions, greening their buildings and taking a myriad personal decisions to do whatever is in their power – and they recognise the frail limitations of that power – to alleviate the catastrophic situation facing the world community.

It doesn't take much imagination to spot the similarities between this crisis and the emergency that faces humanity at a time of world war. All the causes and elements are the same: greed; selfishness; lack of respect for others; a wish to put wealth ahead of human rights; a need to cover up the truth; a profound desire to look the other way.

So in the spirit of Gandhi, Quakers are putting one foot in front of the other and tackling global warming in tiny and insignificant ways that may accumulate to make a difference. And they have a wider vision. They foresee a future in which nation could be fighting nation for natural resources: water, food, living space. They believe that their message of tolerance and peace is more urgently needed than ever, as the world increasingly understands that open-heartedness and generosity will be necessary in sharing all that we have for the common good.

As the need to reduce demands on the earth's resources becomes ever more urgent, people are increasingly bewildered by the data, the propaganda and the inertia of governments. Quaker organisations work with each other and with faith groups of all kinds to establish thoughtful, effective approaches to sustainability. Quaker Earthcare Witness and Friends

Committee on National Legislation in the US, Quaker Peace and Social Witness and Living Witness in the UK, and Quaker Earthcare Committee in Australia, along with many other groups around the world, work to provide analysis, advice and practical help to Quakers as they strive to become a low-carbon sustainable community.

The themes of this chapter and the previous one – **equality, truth, simplicity, peace, sustainability** – are more than mere aspects of the Quaker character. They are five keynotes of the Quaker way: action points (the word often used is "testimonies") that Quakers attempt to put into practice every day.

The list sounds daunting and ambitious, and it is. But each of the five themes overlaps the others and can be put into practice in the multitude of activities, behaviours, attitudes, enthusiasms – even employment choices – that characterise our everyday lives.

And none of this has to be perfect. It's important to reiterate that Quakers are not saints. When they mess up they have learned to be kind to themselves. Putting one foot in front of the other is enough.

Here are some more keynotes of this Quaker way:

Quakers believe that *Thou shalt not kill* means exactly what it says.

Quakers reject the notion that war is inevitable, regarding it always as a failure.

Quakers support the right to conscientious objection, both to fighting in a war and to paying for it.

Quakers campaign for nuclear disarmament and to end the arms trade.

Quakers feel no enmity towards members of the armed forces.

Quakers believe that education on peace and climate change is vital for the future of the planet.

Quakers do not believe that we own the world, or that its resources are ours to dispose of at will.

Quakers are doing all they can to become a low-carbon, sustainable community.

I'll end this chapter with a brief extract from an open letter to King Charles II written by Quakers in 1660. It was their first ever peace declaration. It took them around fifteen years to reach a communal decision to reject warfare and, when they finally did, they were unequivocal about it.

All bloody principles and practices we do utterly deny, with all outward wars, and strife, and fightings with outward weapons, for any end, or under any pretence whatsoever, and this is our testimony to the whole world.

6

Belief, Advice and Awkward Questions

I'm more comfortable with doubt than with certainty. I'm deeply sceptical about Biblical infallibility. I don't know if God's really there and I'm content not to know. And Quakerism allows me to be comfortable with that. It doesn't tell me what to believe. It tells me that I'm welcome to keep thinking. It tells me that I'll be supported.
Chloe Scaling

What do Quakers regard as their Holy Book?

It's a good question, entirely understandable, often asked. It intrigues people. The Bible perhaps? Or the Bhagavad Gita? The Buddhist Scriptures?

You may have absorbed enough about Quakers by now to make a guess. The answer is: all of them and none.

Quakers regard each of them as holy books (not Holy Books) and use them as they think fit. I suppose some Quakers may choose never to read any, but it would be an odd decision if they did, because an intrinsic element of this creedless group is that everyone expects everyone else to be working steadily, quietly on their spiritual lives. And for most of them that means reading old scriptures, kindling new ideas and keeping up with developments in the thinking of other religious communities as well as their own – all part of the process of living faithfully without a creed.

Let's return briefly to this matter of creeds and why Quakers choose to disregard them. Their instinct to base their belief on experience is a crucial factor, but it's not the whole story. They have a deep antipathy towards the very idea of creeds and a particular distaste for the notion that religious unity depends on everyone facing the same way, saying the same thing at the same time.

Creeds give people answers before they've thought of the questions. The implicit message of a creed is, "We've worked out your beliefs, so you don't have to." And the desired result is a group who are in lockstep with one other.

Quakers offer a different kind of discipline and a more personal one: working things out for themselves, knowing they'll never find easy answers, contemplating the great mysteries for the sheer love and uncertainty and compulsion of it, and then letting the energy of that experience inspire them to work for the good of others. It's just as resilient as a morality learned from a list of beliefs, but it's also individual, exhilarating and born of an open mind.

Quaker libraries – just about every meeting house has its own – are likely to have copies of the Bible in many of its translations, and quite possibly the Koran, the Tao and the Hindu scriptures, as well as other religious books intended to interest and challenge their communities. The Bible, in particular, is of vital importance to many Quakers. It is on the central table at most meetings, and the New Testament remains a core Quaker text, even for those who don't declare themselves to be Christians.

Quakers have been publishing since they began. In their earliest days in seventeenth-century England they produced endless leaflets explaining themselves; then, when their enemies hit back with an identical number denouncing them as hypocrites and fools, the Quakers replied with still more. It was a heady, passionate time and the literature it produced makes fascinating reading for anyone prepared to negotiate its occasional eccentricities of style.

Finding out about other people's religious lives can be curiously helpful in sorting out your own. From the beginning, Quakers published what they called "journals" – spiritual autobiographies in which they explored their conversion to Quakerism (they described it as their "convincement") and told the story of what happened next. George Fox's *Journal* is still read widely by Quakers and non-Quakers alike for the extraordinary rough-and-tumble of his life and the moral wisdom of his thought. And similarly the *Journal* of John Woolman, a prophetic, compassionate and utterly committed North American Quaker, has never lost its capacity to inspire readers of all religious backgrounds and none.

Quakers today write books, magazine articles and blogs in surprising numbers for such a comparatively small group, but their main sources of inspiration are the communally produced volumes of guidance and advice that are often placed on the central table at their meetings. Usually called *Faith and Practice*, or a variation on that theme, and revised every thirty years or so to ensure that they can't become museum pieces, they are beautifully curated anthologies of Quaker wisdom and experience.

Each country (or, in the USA, each large region) publishes a version for their own people. Quakers don't have a central decision-making body – each group is autonomous and no group defers to any other – so there are differences between the various editions.

Quakers usually have a soft spot for the version they discovered first. As a British Quaker I feel particular affection for the one published in the UK called *Quaker Faith & Practice*, but I also have great fondness for *Faith and Practice*, produced in California by Pacific Yearly Meeting, and *This We Can Say*, a wise and idiosyncratic anthology published by Quakers in Australia. There are many more.

It is in these and the other similar volumes that Quaker belief and practice are most eloquently explored. If you're interested, you might find it worth your while to check out the edition for your nation or area. You'll rarely encounter such a remarkable combination of compelling writing and authentic religious experience. And, because the books are produced locally and cover Quakerism up to the present day, you could find yourself sitting in a meeting next to one of the authors you most admire. As a Quaker of my acquaintance once said, "I love it, because it really is *our* book."

Riffle through it, read extracts at random, and you will appreciate the scope and variety of its contents.

There are descriptions of what a Quaker meeting might mean to its members,

Our life is love, and peace, and tenderness; and bearing one with another, and forgiving one another, and not laying accusations one against another; but praying one for another, and helping one another up with a tender hand. (Isaac Penington, 1667)

reminders of what Quaker communities are for,

Meet together and know one another in that which is eternal, which was before the world was. (George Fox, 1657)

thoughts about the undercurrents in Quakers' spiritual practice,

When one rises to speak in a meeting one has a sense of being used, of being played upon, of being spoken through. (Thomas R Kelly, 1966)

explorations of personal experience,

I was terrified I'd break down.
I did.
It didn't matter. (Rosalind M Baker, 1986)

advice around Quaker simplicity,

[These] should not be viewed as laws but as one attempt

to flesh out the meaning of simplicity. ... First, buy things for their usefulness rather than their status. Second, reject anything that is producing an addiction in you. Third, develop a habit of giving things away. De-accumulate. Fourth, refuse to be propagandised by the custodians of modern gadgetry. Fifth, learn to enjoy things without owning them. Sixth, develop a deeper appreciation for the creation. Seventh, look with a healthy scepticism at all "buy now, pay later" schemes. Eighth, obey Jesus' injunction about plain, honest speech. Ninth, reject anything that will breed the oppression of others. Tenth, shun whatever would distract you from your main goal. (Richard J Foster, 1979)

thoughts on peace,

A good end cannot sanctify evil means; nor must we ever do evil, that good may come of it. (William Penn, 1693)

Conscientious objection is not a total repudiation of force; it is a refusal to surrender moral responsibility for one's action. (Kenneth C Barnes, 1987)

and more, including material about the personal journeys of Quakers; reflections on close relationships; pieces on prayer, conflict, social responsibility, family dynamics; chapters on the running of Quaker meetings; and a unique section intended to help Quakers with the blessings and challenges of everyday life, called, in most editions at least, Advices and Queries.

Advices and Queries is what it says it is: pieces of advice and some very good questions. An introductory paragraph to the British version (published as a separate booklet and given away free) describes it as being "for the comfort and discomfort" of Quakers. That's exactly right. Some of the queries, in particular, can cause people to shift uneasily in their seats.

Are you honest and truthful in all you say and do?

Do you dwell too much on the hope of recognition or reward?

Are you working to bring about a just and compassionate society?

What unpalatable truths might you be evading?

Awkward questions, all of them, and there are more, with no easy answers for anyone.

If pressure is brought on you to lower your standard of integrity, are you prepared to resist it?

Do you keep yourself informed about the effects your style of living is having on the global economy and environment?

Are you able to contemplate your death and the death of those closest to you?

Nothing here constitutes a Quaker belief, but each has a fundamental principle of Quakerism at its heart. And the question mark ensures that there isn't anything fixed or final about them.

The fact that Quakers think these questions are worth asking and, more importantly, that they are prepared to spend time contemplating what their own answers might be, tells you something about them. They don't feel guilt or shame if they find a query discomforting. They simply use their unease as a stimulant to action and change.

The advices work in the same way. Here are some snatches, again from the British version.

Live adventurously.

Seek to know an inward stillness, even amid the activities of daily life.

Approach old age with courage and hope.

Consider which of the ways to happiness offered by society

are truly fulfilling and which are potentially corrupting and destructive.

Refrain from making prejudiced judgements about the life journeys of others.

Try reading the next paragraph – it's from Advice 17 of the British edition – with a pause between each sentence. Is there anything for you here?

When words are strange or disturbing to you, try to sense where they come from and what has nourished the lives of others. Listen patiently and seek the truth which other people's opinions may contain for you. Avoid hurtful criticism and provocative language. Do not allow the strength of your convictions to betray you into making statements or allegations that are unfair or untrue. Think it possible that you may be mistaken.

It is intended as advice for Quakers, but it might be mistaken for a description of them. And it is advice that can help newcomers, because it gives a sense of the balance that Quakers look for in everything. They are passionate and vociferous in their commitment to campaigning for peace and social justice – they march and protest and commit acts of civil disobedience – but respect for others is equally essential to a life based on truth and equality.

If you want ritual, or a formula for life, or a book of rules, they have little to offer; but it would be a mistake to assume that Quakers lack rigour. They make frequent demands of each other, not least in their tacit assumption that everyone in their community will be engaged in discovering themselves and what they believe. *Faith and Practice* and *Advices and Queries* provide a framework and a discipline that help them do it. The purpose of both books is to support people as they undertake the changes they aspire to, and cope with the ones that take them by surprise. It's the nearest Quakers get to telling people how to live their lives.

Their hands-off approach often leads to accusations that Quakerism is a "pick-and-mix", "do-it-yourself" religion in which people can believe anything they like. And they themselves have been known to fret that too much leeway might eventually cause them to lack direction and purpose. But those worries ignore the strength of Quakers' spiritual practice.

If people keep turning up to Quaker meetings to explore the Inner Light, and if that Light stays with them in their work and family lives, and if they respond to the promptings of love and truth they experience as a result, *their lives will change*. It won't happen overnight. It might take weeks or months. But it will happen. It happens all the time. And the result will not be a group of people who believe what they like.

Quakers don't believe what they like. As a result of their experience Quakers believe what they must.

7

Identity, Community

I don't think Quakerism is a religion. I think it's a religious society.
John Shinebourne

"Quaker" started as an insult. In seventeenth-century England it was unthinkable to agree with them that hierarchies should be abolished. Not only that, it was criminal to suggest that you could become a priest if you hadn't been to a university and heretical to believe in an Inner Light in everyone. Yet hundreds of converts to this new religious faith took to the streets, risking their lives to proclaim their conviction that the Divine was at work inside them. They trembled, quivered and quaked in the bliss of their religious ecstasy and were widely abused as mere "quakers". The name stuck. It wasn't long before everyone started to spell it with a capital "Q".

The heretics and their critics calmed down over the years and the insults were largely forgotten. "Quaker" evolved into a something friendlier, just a nickname, and the word became accepted, even acceptable. And by the early nineteenth century it was being used as an alternative to a more formal designation: "The Religious Society of Friends". So "Quaker" and "Friend" came to mean the same thing. They still do today.

Whichever you choose depends on how you feel. I've used "Quaker" throughout this book because at the time of writing it's the word people are most familiar with. And "Friend" has too many associations to be explicit. It was originally used as a shortening of "Friends of the Truth", but that has lost its significance with the years. And since "Friends" is used as a title for everything from songs to plays to TV shows, its power to stand out from the crowd is diminished.

Quakers still use it among themselves. They call each other "Friend" – which looks odd in print, but in practice is expressive and heartfelt – and the word turns up all the time in the names of Quaker organisations: committees, schools, trusts and charities. The official title of the Quaker community as a whole now contains both words: The Religious Society of Friends (Quakers).

Quakers aren't good at updating the language they use, and that word "Society" needs explaining. I have a feeling that its clubby overtones may be partly responsible for the notion that Quakers are a closed group, so it's worth repeating that they do all they can to welcome everybody equally at their meetings. Anyone can turn up, whoever they are, whatever their reason, and visitors are considered to be integral contributors to the life of the group for as long as they want to be.

Why "Society"? Because you can join. There's a system of membership. Someone who comes week after week without wanting any formal affiliation is called an "attender". If the same person eventually decides they are committed to Quakers, they become a "member". So it is, broadly speaking, a society.

The idea dates from the early days when no one quite knew which people in their groups were committed to Quakerism and which were dipping a toe in the Quaker water. Membership involves giving money and time, as much as each person can afford, because those are the two essentials required in keeping the organisation going. Some people report a change of attitude when they join – it can feel like a spiritual awakening – while others don't notice much difference.

Many people keep coming without having any desire to register their commitment. A few take a long time to make the decision. Others decide to become members after a year or two. It's rare for someone to join a Quaker community and then change their mind, but it does happen; in which case they are entirely free to leave.

Community matters to Quakers. Their groups are confusingly

called "meetings" – the same word as the one they use for their spiritual practice, so I'll continue referring to them as "groups" – and are organised independently from one another, coming together often for regional and national gatherings and also, from time to time, holding a large world-wide convocation.

The ways in which Quakers administer their communities and handle their business are unconventional to a degree that astonishes newcomers. People wonder how they can possibly manage their affairs without any hierarchy, without anyone being in charge, and, perhaps most amazingly, without ever taking a vote. But they do. And it works. It works so well, in fact, that Quakers are sometimes asked to teach their decision-making techniques to organisations that have no Quaker presence at all. Perhaps they could work for you.

I'll explain them.

First, how to manage without a hierarchy.

Quakers operate a system of three-year terms, so people do their jobs voluntarily for just three years at a time. If they want to continue after those three – and if the group wishes them to carry on – they serve a second term, making six years in all. Then they are asked to stop and do something else.

Rotating the jobs is a good system so long as everyone understands it. People sometimes need to be reminded that going from a role of great responsibility to something more menial isn't demotion, it's just moving things around. And when they consider the reasoning behind the process, the accompanying diminution of "me-me" thinking comes as a relief rather than a penance. No worry that someone else is better, or faster, or cleverer. No jockeying for position. The expertise you gain this time will be of use somewhere else next time. All the talents are being used and the community is being strengthened by nurturing the skills of everyone.

The jobs that need doing are reminiscent of those in other religious organisations, but not the same. The Clerk, for example, looks at first sight like some kind of Quaker-style priest-in-charge, and there are Elders, too, who might be mistaken for the same thing. But nothing could be further from the truth. Everybody is a priest. No one is in charge.

The Clerk acts as a conduit for everyone's concerns, suggestions, worries and plans. Business meetings are "chaired" by the Clerk in a way unique to Quakers, which I'll explain shortly. The Elders are responsible for the spiritual life of the group for their three-year term, making sure that meetings are properly held and acting as a helpful ear at times of personal crisis.

There are people whose specific responsibility is pastoral care: everything from sending birthday cards to young Quakers, to making arrangements for the Quaker meetings held around hospital beds. There are also some whose job is to ensure that the fabric of the building is maintained, others who care for the group's children. There are librarians, treasurers, caterers, welcomers, newsletter editors and trustees.

Who gives all these people these three-yearly jobs? The answer is the group as a whole. And how does that work? It happens through the structure and method of Quaker business meetings. So that is where I'll turn next.

Quakers' business meetings are held in precisely the same way as their other meetings. That means they are based on silence and stillness. Some people see it as a drawback that they tend to be slow, but slowness is one of the factors that give them their integrity. And in that spirit I intend taking my explanation slowly, too.

When the meeting is ready to begin, everyone drops into silence. For secular groups this period of quiet – five, ten, perhaps fifteen minutes – serves as a useful pause to refresh the mind. In the case of Quakers it does that, while also working in the same way as it does for their other meetings, focusing the mind and spirit on the Inner Light.

Continuing in the stillness, the Clerk quietly announces the first issue that the group is to discuss and the meeting gets under way. More silence. Considered, fertile silence. The Clerk watches to see if any mood is discernible around the group. Someone stands. He speaks his mind as thoughtfully, clearly and succinctly as he can. More silence. Another person stands and speaks. The Clerk is beginning to note down key words and ideas in what is being said. More silence. More people stand to speak, one by one.

This method of discussing matters of business is based on careful listening. Everyone is listening attentively, openly. They haven't gone in with their own agenda – or if they have, the initial silence has put paid to it – and now they are hearing what everyone has to say. The speakers are expressing views, but nothing is pre-packaged or preached. There are no interruptions or exchanges. Each person is speaking in turn. This isn't a debate. And it isn't necessarily heavy, either – business meetings are often surprisingly entertaining and can be an unexpected source of laughter, sunshine and good humour.

The Clerk listens with a particular purpose: to discern what Quakers call "the sense of the meeting". What are these people saying? Are they reaching some kind of a conclusion together? If not, everyone should continue to speak into the silence. If so, the Clerk asks for quiet in order to write a minute – a record of their decision – there and then.

This is a critical difference between the Quaker way of handling a committee meeting and the way of the world. Quaker minutes are written during the meeting, in the moment, while it's happening. They can't be fixed afterwards. Once the Clerk decides that the meeting is reaching unity on the matter in question, she writes a minute, recording a decision, and reads it out. At that stage, anyone can question any choice of words, request rewrites, suggest changes – in the final analysis it's the group's minute, not the Clerk's. Once the minute is complete it is read out, accepted by the group and put into practice by everyone, including those who weren't present when the decision was taken.

Every Quaker has stories of going into a meeting convinced of the rightness of one point of view, only to light on another more harmonious one – not through oratory or powers of persuasion, but by tranquil reflection in the stillness. No adversarial language. No arguing. No voting. The quiet integrity of a Quaker business meeting can be startlingly beautiful.

Who appoints people to their roles? It's the whole group, using these same techniques. First, they appoint a committee to think about the vacancies that need to be filled and the names of suitable people. When they have done that, they take the list back to the larger group, who give it due consideration. And so when the three-yearly appointments are finally made, it's been the whole group doing the appointing.

I say the whole group, but that is to leave out something that is experienced by all Quakers at some time in their lives and by most of them most weeks: a sense of being guided. Some people put it down to simple group psychology, but a greater number think that something else is going on, a feeling of being led, pushed sometimes, by the Light inside them to reach decisions that are innovative and unexpected. For many, this force – for that is what it is – is the element that gives silent Quaker meetings their uncommon power.

Quakers today are quieter than their seventeenth-century forebears, but they do understand what it is to quake. There isn't a regular visitor to Quaker meetings who doesn't recognise the shudder in the heart or the restless quiver in the limbs when a new inspiration hits them. It may not be the violent juddering of their ancestors, but they know it well enough. It's real.

In the next chapter I'll ask some Quakers to talk about their experience. Meanwhile, let's draw together a few of the themes of this one.

Listening with attentiveness and love is at the heart of Quakerism and lies at the core of Quakers' business meetings.

Quaker business meetings can't be controlled by rhetoric or the power of personality.

It is impossible to determine the outcome of a Quaker business meeting in advance or change its decisions afterwards.

Quaker business meetings are based on integrity and transparency.

Quakers still quake.

8

Everyday Quakers

Quakerism is a place for searchers, people who are looking for something – looking to find out if they can make sense of this life we all pass through.
Rajan Naidu

It's time to meet some Quakers. I've assembled a group of eight of varying ages and backgrounds, and recorded conversations with them. Here are some extracts. Dip in and out of them as you please. Listening to snatches of experience and belief can be a good way to find out more.

The youngest person is twenty-one, the oldest eighty-seven. They include a student, an actor, an engineer and the former CEO of a charity that supports and promotes the work of peacemakers.

Their religious backgrounds, too, are varied. Two of them were brought up as Quakers, another two as Anglicans. Of the remaining four, one was a Methodist, another a Roman Catholic, the third was born into the Jewish faith, and the fourth was raised by Hindus.

Six of them are members of the Religious Society of Friends. The other two have decided, for the foreseeable future at least, not to join. They all identify as Quakers.

They are: Kelly Burke, Carolyn Hayman, David Henshaw, Maya Metheven, Rajan Naidu, Chloe Scaling, John Shinebourne and Frank Treviss. You may recognise their names, because I've already quoted from them at the opening of each chapter.

oOo

John: I went to my first Quaker meeting when I was at university. It bowled me over. This silence – it wasn't an absence of noise, it was an attentiveness to some sort of presence. I felt there's something to this.

Chloe: I've been going to Quaker meetings for just over a year now and I joined the Religious Society of Friends six weeks ago. To start with, I struggled to get through an hour of silence without wondering what I was going to have for lunch. But after a while I found it really valuable and I've made a lot of good friends. It's one of the best decisions I've ever made.

Maya: I've always been a Quaker, because my mum's a Quaker, and I went every week, so I can't remember my first meeting. I stopped going for about three years after university, then started again when I moved to London. What brought me back was the space and the silence and the community, and also knowing that other Quakers are active and working for social change. I wanted to be with people who do that. So that's what led me back into Quakerism.

Rajan: I didn't know what to expect. There were people sitting, about forty or fifty people, in a circle in this room. There was just a table with a couple of books on it, some flowers. No pictures on the wall, nothing. I didn't expect that. I thought there would be some kind of icon, but there was nothing. It was a new experience to be in a room with other people. To be in stillness with others who are sharing the same space, trying not to distract one another, integrated with other people, other people integrated with you. You become part of them, they become part of you. It's unspoken, hard to put into words. It made quite an impact on me.

Frank: I loved the ambience of my first meeting. I loved the silence. I found an hour a bit too long to start with, but now I find it far too short. And I've been going almost every week since. Wherever I am in the world I always do all I can to find a Quaker meeting, because I always need it.

David: I had a boyfriend in London and one Sunday morning over breakfast he said, "I'm going to a Quaker meeting, do you want to come?" And so I found myself at Westminster Meeting House, sitting in this rather solemn, quiet place. But it seemed *all right.* There were interesting people there, and one or two of them spoke in the meeting. And when we came away my boyfriend said to me, "What did you make of that, then?" I said, "Yeah, there's something in that, I might come back to it." I thought I'd get on with my life and maybe add it on afterwards – and that's exactly what I did, but, alas, some forty-five years later. It was one Christmas Day. I was spending Christmas on my own as I usually do and I thought, "I'll go along and see what this is all about." And I went to a Quaker meeting. And I went the next week. And I've gone almost every week since. It convinced me immediately that this was where I needed to be. I was seventy-six.

Chloe: More often than not it's just a chance to pause and reflect on the week, but sometimes it's much more of a religious experience. I feel a kind of warming in my chest. I feel the presence of what I suppose I might call the Inner Light. I visualise it as a ball of light, the size of my fist, in the centre of my chest, next to my heart. Sometimes I've physically felt some kind of presence there and I've been moved to speak.

Carolyn: Something happens when you stand up to speak in a Quaker meeting that's different from what happens in other settings. You don't want to stand up, but you find you *are* standing up. Whatever you call it – the Light within, the Spirit – something is moving you, something is working on you to make it happen.

Kelly: In my first meeting a man stood up in the silence and said, "What is it about robins? I saw one this morning on my window sill and I was inexplicably comforted." That was all he said. And I'd always secretly believed that God – I still say God, because it's a word from my former Catholicism and it kind of stands in for what I mean – I'd always secretly believed that God exists in the small things.

David: Things happen to me in Quaker meetings. It isn't just in the meeting itself. It's in the preparation. The day before, I'm thinking about what issue I'm taking to the meeting, and two days afterwards, I'm thinking. "Oh my God, that's exactly the problem I took to the meeting" – and I've got the answer! It feels like a whirlwind. I'm able to work something out and it falls into place and the answer's there. Answers sometimes come like a shot of light while I'm actually in the meeting. I see this metaphorical bright light. "Oh, that's what I must do." Or, "That's what I must say to move things on." Or, "That's what I can offer by way of support."

John: It isn't meditation. When people meditate they are drawn into an individualised personal space. They're screening things out, rather than letting things in. A Quaker meeting is a place to let things in, not screen things out. If I want to do something for myself I can do it by myself. I don't need to go to a meeting. What I need to feel is both *included* and *including* of everyone who is there.

Carolyn: I remember once I was angry with someone because I felt I'd been treated very badly. And I came into meeting and the words "filled with grace" just came into my head. I realised that I couldn't be filled with grace and be keeping on with this anger. And it floated away like a balloon. It was gone. It was something I'd been chewing over for months.

Rajan: Sometimes I don't feel like going to a Quaker meeting for one reason or another, but I try to go anyway, and often I've found that just being there can be very constructive. Something moves me, or strikes me, or rings a bell with me. It's happened many times.

Chloe: When I first got to Quakers I used to read *Advices & Queries*, and I'd start at the beginning, but I'd just stop there. I didn't want to go any further. I'd just concentrate on the first few words. It was as if they reached out a hand to me.

Frank: The Quakers have changed me. I used to be a bit right-wing. I'd been indoctrinated by my upbringing. I believed in capital punishment, I was homophobic, I had a militaristic attitude. When something came up on the news I thought, "Send in the British army, they'll sort it out." After I left school I was apprenticed to an engineering firm, so I wasn't rich, and I was trying to get a family together, and the only way I could see of making money was to work really hard and adopt a right-wing attitude. Not being generous to other people, being selfish, keeping it all to myself and condemning people who were on the dole. But finding Quakers caused me to change my attitude and opinions towards community and government, and my political views have totally changed. I've learned about kindness and compassion and how to offer them to others. When I joined Quakers I put the brakes on. I sat in the stillness and began to think about other people and how I could help them.

Maya: It helps to have had Quakerism in my life all the way through. At eighteen I was in Peru on my own, travelling. I don't think that would have happened without the Quakers. Being aware of the world, the challenge of wanting to see for myself rather than accepting what I've been told, that's a particularly Quaker narrative. Having Quakerism in my life has always taught me to question, ask a bit more, go a bit deeper. And going to Young Quaker Summer Schools as a teenager gave me the confidence to go off and do things on my own, away from my parents. Other kids at school didn't manage to do that.

Carolyn: Quaker meetings set me on the next path. So I'm always thinking: "What's the next thing I need to do? Use my money in a different way? Live in a different way? Why am I living a comfortable life when I could be doing so much more to mend the world?"

John: When I first came to Quakers I liked what I was reading about the Inward Light, about life as a sacrament. The sacrament *is* life – there's no need for any other sacrament, other than the recognition that the life you've been given *is* the sacrament for you, for you as an individual. And of course, for every other individual, for every other person.

Kelly: I felt like the Quakers were basically saying, "There's no difference between your spiritual and your secular life. We have testimonies to sustainability, truth, simplicity, equality and peace, but your experience of God is your own. We'll sit here in silence and we'll support each other's spiritual journeys by lending energy and support." And I said to myself, "These are my people!", because it was what I'd always thought: there's no difference between my spiritual life in church and my spiritual life out of church.

Rajan: Quakerism is all about the work. It's very exciting. The way people are treated in prisons, human rights violations, homelessness, mental health issues, peacemaking, diplomacy. These are what Quakers are strong on and can give a lead to the world.

Chloe: Equality leads to peace, and it leads to truth and integrity. And equality and simplicity are linked as well. I think sustainability should be seen separately from the others, because it's such a priority for the world. And it's an encouragement to me that Quakers highlight it so much.

Carolyn: One of the reasons I took a long time to become a member was that I found that it was very difficult to tell the strict truth in the venture capital industry, where I worked for several years. In that environment everything was always made out to be slightly bigger than it really was. I wouldn't ever say that we'd got an order for software if we hadn't, but I might say we had several major animation studios looking at our software when maybe it was two. And I wasn't strong enough or principled enough to be straight down the line in telling them the absolute truth.

Kelly: Simplicity doesn't necessarily mean not having

anything. Having too little doesn't allow you to live simply and I know that from experience. I understand simplicity as a lack of noise: removing the extraneous things that distract me from working with clarity.

Maya: I was at Bradford University in the Peace Studies Department, which was set up by Quakers. In my first week I missed lectures, went up to Faslane Peace Camp in Scotland and got arrested. So I definitely went into it with a sense of *being* my beliefs.

Carolyn: If you're well you may never think about good health, but the minute you're ill it's the one thing you want. It's the same with peace. If you've got peace you don't even know you've got it. And the minute your daughter can't go out into the street without the possibility of being bombed or abducted, it's the only thing you want. So if you think peace is not a priority it's a failure of your imagination.

John: Being a Quaker prison chaplain deepened my faith. It was the best work I've ever done anywhere. I was able to start a Quaker meeting of twelve, thirteen, fourteen people. It was good to be in a team of other chaplains. They were Sikh, Muslim, Anglican, Hindu, lovely people. And we had an open-hearted Catholic managing chaplain – without him, nothing would have been possible for me. I discovered from my work in prison that if you treat someone with respect it has an amazing effect on them, particularly when they're not expecting to be treated that way.

Rajan: What do Quakers have in common? Well, a sense of community is one of the things that jumps out of Quakerism for me. Being recognised. Being valued. Being able to make a contribution. Having this intimate connection with a large number of people. The boundaries are very relaxed, very open.

Frank: I've come to understand that love is a natural phenomenon, but hate has to be learned. We need to overcome hate to create community.

Carolyn: The first purpose of life is to enjoy and be thankful for the good things that are set around us. It's a bit like the Christian parable about the person who gives the feast and nobody wants to come – if you spend your life feeling miserable and guilty and hopeless you're ignoring the feast. And if you take pleasure in the feast – family and nature and music and all those things – then you're much more able to do the second thing, which is to mend the world.

Kelly: I'm often in situations where I have to think on the spot, when somebody wants important information from me and they want it quickly. My experience with Quakers has given me the self-confidence to take time in those moments, and not feel that I have to say *something* for the sake of filling a space. It gives me the time to compose my thoughts and make sure that what I say is in line with what I really think.

Maya: It can be hard for people who go to meetings to say what Quakerism is and what it isn't. Yet by defining it too much we can make it harder for others to join in, and for Quakerism to develop and grow and change.

David: Becoming a Quaker made me more certain, more clear-cut. It was the threshold for me of realising the truth that Heaven is here now. We make it. It is something that comes out of everyday life. The medieval concept of it being in a separate place, in another direction, has been a huge disservice to us all. People don't realise that Heaven is here, it's waiting for you. It's like unlocking a door. It's like coming out of a long tunnel into the light, into the brightness, the vividness, the greenness. Heaven is here now, with us, whenever we want it.

oOo

It was not a scientifically chosen selection of Quakers and not a typical one – as we've seen, there's no such thing as a typical Quaker. A scientific sample would be much larger and would need to include at least one committed atheist, a professional in the field of science or medicine, a person with no particular interest in social justice and another living an active life based on nothing else. But these eight are a varied group and the experience they've had and the views they've expressed are by no means uncommon among contemporary Quakers.

I invited them to tell me what Quakers believe. They were all clear that they have as many individual beliefs as anyone else, but no corporate belief system. "We put our emphasis on what a person can say out of their experience," said one, and the others agreed.

They confirmed a long-held opinion of mine that Quakers don't necessarily consider beliefs to be the most important factor in a person's religious life. They are more interested in the doing than the believing.

"What I believe changes over time, probably changes every day," observed one. "Quakers believe that what is true about the spiritual life is true for everyone, but each individual has to find their own way," said another.

So if you look to Quakers for a belief system you are going to be disappointed. They have learned to trust the promptings of love and truth in their hearts as the leadings of God. They base their lives on an outpouring of impulses and ideas that is different for each person, and they only believe what they have experienced. Without the oxygen of experience, Quakers regard belief as inert, like a butterfly impaled on a pin in a glass case: beautiful but lifeless.

Many Quakers share the unwillingness to define Quakerism that Maya Metheven expresses in her last contribution. Yet, like her, they sympathise with people who find it difficult to pin Quakers down to a set of beliefs that can be easily digested. If I've done nothing else in this book, though, I hope I've shown that anybody who finds the motivation to turn up at half-a-dozen meetings will find Quakerism easy enough to absorb.

I'll finish with a truth spoken by David Henshaw in his final contribution. "Heaven is here now," he says. "We make it. It is something that comes out of everyday life."

The original Quakers of three-and-a-half centuries ago trusted that it might be possible to build what they called "the kingdom" into the everyday life of each person on the planet. Quakers today rarely use such language, but they share the impulse to work for social and spiritual change, and to help build a society inspired by the promptings of love and truth in every heart. Many of them call it "mending the world".

Quakers know that the kingdom, enlightenment, heaven, call it what you will, lies firmly within the grasp of human beings. They know it because they've seen the personal transformation that can take hold of people who spend time sitting together in stillness.

So I'm adding one last belief to the others that I've highlighted in this book. As with the others, it's a belief based entirely on the personal experience of Quakers. As with the others, I'm not adding it as a Quaker spokesperson – there's no such thing – but as an impassioned observer. And, as with the others, I'm adding it with confidence, with enthusiasm and in bold:

Heaven is here now. We make it. It is something that comes out of everyday life.

About the Author

Geoffrey Durham went to his first Quaker meeting in 1994 and has been going regularly ever since. He worked as an entertainer, actor and director for thirty-five years before retiring in 2006 to work more actively for Quakers. He was one of the founders of Quaker Quest, a groundbreaking outreach project, was an editor and contributor to the *Twelve Quakers* series of books (republished by O-Books as *New Light*) and has twice been a Quaker presence on Radio 4's *Thought for the Day*. He has written three introductions to Quakerism for newcomers and is a regular speaker at Quaker events.

CHRISTIAN
ALTERNATIVE

Christian Alternative

THE NEW OPEN SPACES

Throughout the two thousand years of Christian tradition there have been, and still are, groups and individuals that exist in the margins and upon the edge of faith. But in Christianity's contrapuntal history it has often been these outcasts and pioneers that have forged contemporary orthodoxy out of former radicalism as belief evolves to engage with and encompass the ever-changing social and scientific realities. Real faith lies not in the comfortable certainties of the Orthodox, but somewhere in a half-glimpsed hinterland on the dirt track to Emmaus, where the Death of God meets the Resurrection, where the supernatural Christ meets the historical Jesus, and where the revolution liberates both the oppressed and the oppressors.

Welcome to Christian Alternative... a space at the edge where the light shines through.
If you have enjoyed this book, why not tell other readers by posting a review on your preferred book site.

Recent bestsellers from Christian Alternative are:

Bread Not Stones
The Autobiography of An Eventful Life
Una Kroll
The spiritual autobiography of a truly remarkable woman
and a history of the struggle for ordination in the Church of
England.
Paperback: 978-1-78279-804-0 ebook: 978-1-78279-805-7

The Quaker Way
A Rediscovery
Rex Ambler
Although fairly well known, Quakerism is not well understood.
The purpose of this book is to explain how Quakerism works as
a spiritual practice.
Paperback: 978-1-78099-657-8 ebook: 978-1-78099-658-5

Blue Sky God
The Evolution of Science and Christianity
Don MacGregor
Quantum consciousness, morphic fields and blue-sky
thinking about God and Jesus the Christ.
Paperback: 978-1-84694-937-1 ebook: 978-1-84694-938-8

Celtic Wheel of the Year
Tess Ward
An original and inspiring selection of prayers combining
Christian and Celtic Pagan traditions, and interweaving their
calendars into a single pattern of prayer for every morning
and night of the year.
Paperback: 978-1-90504-795-6

Christian Atheist
Belonging without Believing
Brian Mountford
Christian Atheists don't believe in God but miss him: especially the transcendent beauty of his music, language, ethics, and community.
Paperback: 978-1-84694-439-0 ebook: 978-1-84694-929-6

Compassion Or Apocalypse?
A Comprehensible Guide to the Thoughts of René Girard
James Warren
How René Girard changes the way we think about God and the Bible, and its relevance for our apocalypse-threatened world.
Paperback: 978-1-78279-073-0 ebook: 978-1-78279-072-3

Diary Of A Gay Priest
The Tightrope Walker
Rev. Dr. Malcolm Johnson
Full of anecdotes and amusing stories, but the Church is still a dangerous place for a gay priest.
Paperback: 978-1-78279-002-0 ebook: 978-1-78099-999-9

Do You Need God?
Exploring Different Paths to Spirituality Even For Atheists
Rory J.Q. Barnes
An unbiased guide to the building blocks of spiritual belief.
Paperback: 978-1-78279-380-9 ebook: 978-1-78279-379-3

The Gay Gospels
Good News for Lesbian, Gay, Bisexual, and Transgendered People
Keith Sharpe
This book refutes the idea that the Bible is homophobic and makes visible the gay lives and validated homoerotic

experience to be found in it.

Paperback: 978-1-84694-548-9 ebook: 978-1-78099-063-7

The Illusion of "Truth"

The Real Jesus Behind the Grand Myth

Thomas Nehrer

Nehrer, uniquely aware of Reality's integrated flow, elucidates Jesus' penetrating, often mystifying insights – exposing widespread religious, scholarly and skeptical fallacy.

Paperback: 978-1-78279-548-3 ebook: 978-1-78279-551-3

Do We Need God to be Good?

An Anthropologist Considers the Evidence

C.R. Hallpike

What anthropology shows us about the delusions of New Atheism and Humanism.

Paperback: 978-1-78535-217-1 ebook: 978-1-78535-218-8

Fingerprints of Fire, Footprints of Peace

A Spiritual Manifesto from a Jesus Perspective

Noel Moules

Christian spirituality with attitude. Fourteen provocative pictures, from Radical Mystic to Messianic Anarchist, that explore identity, destiny, values and activism.

Paperback: 978-1-84694-612-7 ebook: 978-1-78099-903-6

Readers of ebooks can buy or view any of these bestsellers by clicking on the live link in the title. Most titles are published in paperback and as an ebook. Paperbacks are available in traditional bookshops. Both print and ebook formats are available online.

Find more titles and sign up to our readers' newsletter at
http://www.johnhuntpublishing.com/christianity
Follow us on Facebook at
https://www.facebook.com/ChristianAlternative